YOU CAN DRAW
MONSTERS
AND OTHER
SCARY THINGS

by Jannie Ho

PICTURE WINDOW BOOKS
a capstone imprint

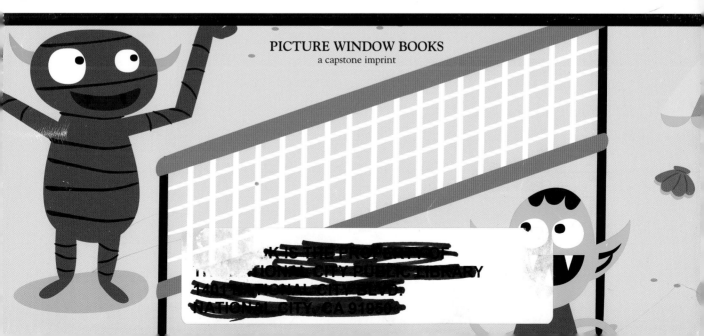

MATERIALS

Before you start your amazing drawings, there are a few things you'll need.

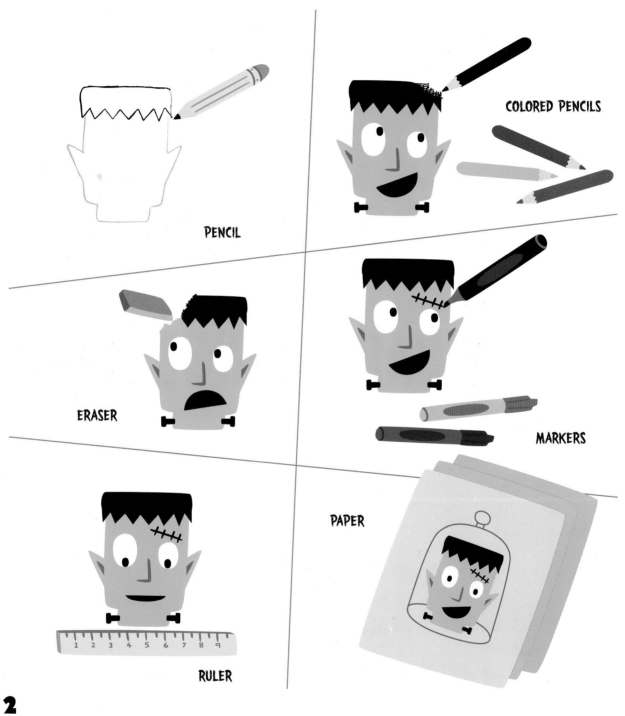

PENCIL

COLORED PENCILS

ERASER

MARKERS

RULER

PAPER

SHAPES

Drawing can be easy! If you can draw these simple letters, numbers, and shapes, YOU CAN DRAW anything in this book.

letters

A B C D
T U W

numbers

1 2 3

shapes

lines

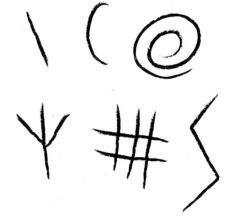

Octo-Monster

Clobber

 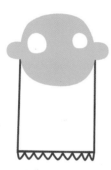  

Gator-Bat

 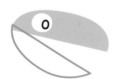  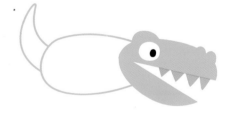

Pinball

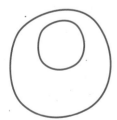   

4

5

Bloodshot

Shaggy

Franken-Fish

Mr. Blob

6

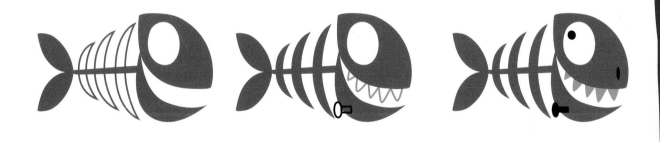

Googly Spider

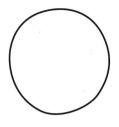 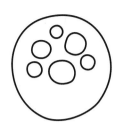  

Finger Freak

Boing-O

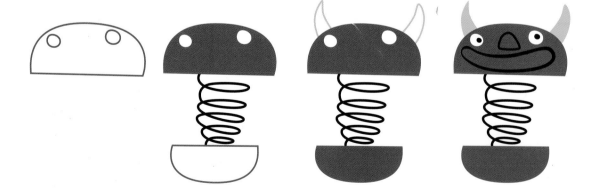

Now try this!

Papa Monster

Baby Mo

Smelly Foot

10

Now try this!

Jack-O'-Lantern

Clawlon

Zeke the Ogre

Feathered Fiend

 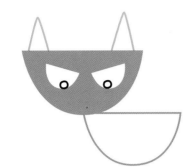 

Nutty Nut

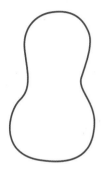 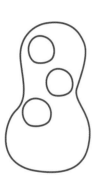  

Funky Chicken

 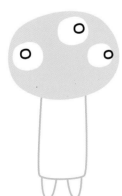  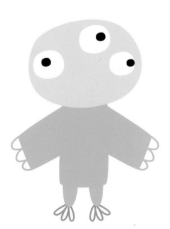

Frankhead

Monstrobot

Crabbo

Venus Flytrap

Medusa

Freaky Tree

Monkey Mummy

Surfboard

Palm Tree

Waves

Swim Fins

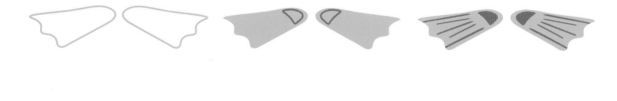

Umbrella

20

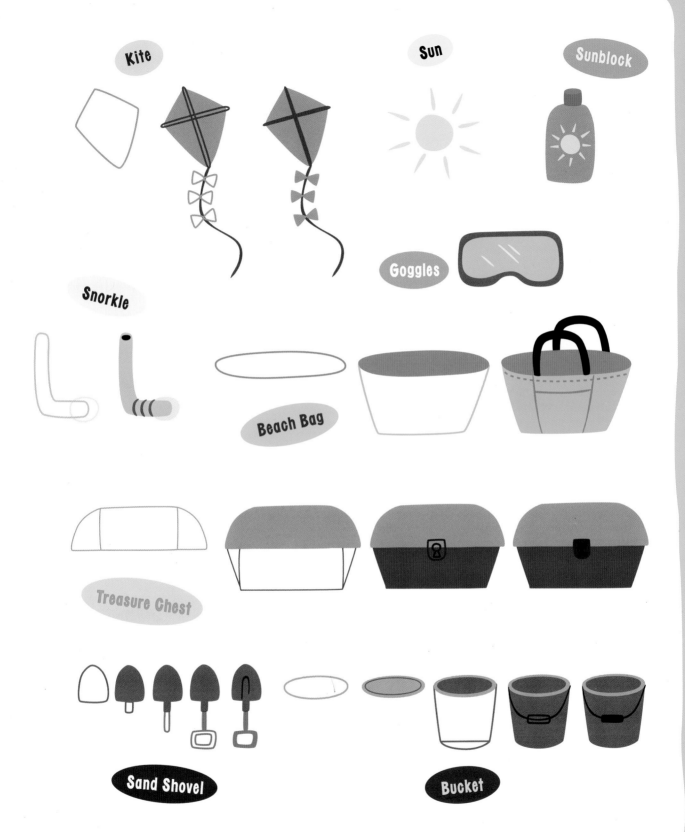

Kite

Sun

Sunblock

Goggles

Snorkle

Beach Bag

Treasure Chest

Sand Shovel

Bucket

21

Library of Congress Cataloging-in-Publication Data
Ho, Jannie
  You can draw monsters and other scary things / by Jannie Ho ;
illustrated by Jannie Ho.
     p. cm. — (You can draw)
  ISBN 978-1-4048-6276-0 (library binding)
  1. Monsters in art—Juvenile literature. 2.
Drawing—Technique—Juvenile literature. I. Ho, Jannie. II. Title.
   NC825.M6B78 2011
   743'.87—dc22

                        2010030029

Printed in the United States of America in North Mankato, Minnesota.
072011
006241R

Picture Window Books
151 Good Counsel Drive
P.O. Box 669
Mankato, MN 56002-0669
877-845-8392
www.capstonepub.com

Editor: Shelly Lyons
Designer: Matt Bruning
Art Director: Nathan Gassman
Production Specialist: Sarah Bennett
The illustrations in this book were created digitally.

Internet Sites •

FactHound offers a safe, fun way to find Internet sites related to this book.
All of the sites on FactHound have been researched by our staff.

Here's all you do:

Visit *www.facthound.com*

Type in this code: 9781404862760

Check out projects, games and lots more at
www.capstonekids.com

Look for all the books in the **You Can Draw** series: